Ukrainian, one day at a time

LANGUAGE LEARNING AND ADVICE FOR ADULTS PLUS PHRASEBOOK FOR USE WITH CHILDREN

Ruth Darby with Aleksandra Mohyl'naya

Ukrainian, one day at a time

For permissions, write to ruth @ spanglishfantastico.com

Profits from the sale of this book will be donated in full to support the work of the Disasters Emergency Committee

Thank you for your purchase.

Ruth Darby with Aleksandra Mohyl'naya

In support of Ukrayiny[1]

A book to help you learn some Ukranian.

Use the video on YouTube to help you with the pronunciation.

Дякую

Dyakuyu

Join in with my reading on YouTube. Search for

"Ukrainian, one day at a time"

on the channel, Learn Ukrainian with me

---

[1] Ukraine

INTRODUCTION

A book to make the Ukrainian language easier to learn.

We can welcome Ukraininan people who arrive in our communities, and one way of doing that is by learning a few words of their language.

Ukrayins'ka[2] is a slavic language. It is not in the same **hrupy**[3] of languages as **anhliys'ka**[4], so there are fewer similarities between **anhliys'koyu ta ukrayins'koyu**[5] than there are between English and German, or **anhliys'koyu ta ispans'koyu**[6]. Because Ukranian is more different for us, it is also more difficult for us. That doesn't mean, however, that **my**[7] can't get these sounds to come out of our mouths; **my**[8] can do it!

Learning a language can be a significant step towards making friends with people who have come **zdaleku**[9]. This book has been written to help you to learn a few words. I did not speak any

---

[2] Ukrainian
[3] group
[4] English
[5] English and Ukrainian
[6] English and Spanish
[7] We … say "mi" in midget
[8] We … mi in midget
[9] From far away

ukrayins'koyu[10] before starting this project, so you are taking a learning journey with me.

Ukrainian is different.

- The alphabet is different
- They don't use words for a and the
- They don't use -s to make things plural
- Nouns have gender
- Nouns change. A lot!
- There are formal and informal words for you.

These differences make learning a bit of Ukrainian challenging, but this is **akt**[11] of friendship to the people of a country who need support at this time.

All profits from the sale of this book go to the Disasters Emergency **Komitetu**[12] to help provide **humanitarnu**[13] aid to those affected by the **konfliktu**[14].

---

[10] Ukrainian … there are variations of this word which almost certainly depend on its role in a given sentence. My advice? Don't worry about it!

[11] An act

[12] Committee

[13] Humanitarian

[14] conflict

Contents

A different alphabet

Ukrayins'ka[15] uses the cyrillic alphabet. You don't have to learn this to speak the words, **ale tse korysnyy instrument**[16]. **Dorosli ukrayintsi**[17] can help you to say the words correctly if they can see what you are saying in print. Here it is, in case you meet a **ukrayintsya**[18] who would like to help you learn the language.

	Ukraninan letter	Roman alphabet	Approximate sound it makes
1	А а	A	a in cat
2	Б б	B	b in boy
3	В в	V	V in vase
4	Г г	H	Between H and G
5	Ґ ґ	G	g in goat
6	Д д	D	d in dog
7	Е е	E	e in egg
8	Є є	ie, ye-	Ye in yellow
9	Ж ж	ž /ʒ/	si in vision
10	З з	Z	z in zoo
11	И и	Y	i in Jasmine

---

[15] Ukrainian
[16] But it is a useful tool
[17] Ukrainian adults
[18] Ukrainian

12	І і	I	I in believe
13	Ї ї	i, yi-	I in pig or yi in yip
14	Й й	i, j, y-	I in pig, j in jam, y in yes
15	К к	K	k in kick
16	Л л	L	l in log
17	М м	M	m in man
18	Н н	N	n in not
19	О о	O	o in not
20	П п	P	p in pig
21	Р р	R	r in ride
22	С с	S	s in set
23	Т т	T	t in ten
24	У у	U	oo in too
25	Ф ф	F	f in fox
26	Х х	Kh	kh in work hard
27	Ц ц	Ts	ts in waits
28	Ч ч	Ch	ch in chip
29	Ш ш	Sh	sh in ship
30	Щ щ	Shch	shch in wa<u>sh</u> <u>ch</u>in
31	Ь ь	/◌ʲ/	Soft sign
32	Ю ю	iu, yu-	you in you
33	Я я	ia, ya-	ya in yam

This is not going to be easy, **ale**[19] I will make it as easy as I can. That means it is not going to be **ideal'nym**[20], but hopefully it's going to be **funktsional'nym**[21]. We can support each other more if we can communicate.

One last thing before we get right into it. You will have noticed that I am including **ukrayins'ki slova**[22] written in the Roman alphabet and embedded **v tekst**[23]. **Bud' laska**[24] sound these out as you read them. The temptation might be to skip over them, **ale**[25] by taking the time to form the words in your mind, you are beginning to learn a little more of the **ukrayins'ku movu**[26]. If you are going to read a book, you might as well read it properly. That way you get the most from it. Having a go is an act of **druzhby ta solidarnosti**[27] towards the Ukranian people.

---

[19] but
[20] perfect
[21] functional
[22] Ukrainian words
[23] In the text
[24] Please
[25] but
[26] Ukrainian language
[27] Friendship and solidarity

Guess Test One

What do you think these words from the text mean?

hrupy
anhliys'ka
zdaleku
akt
konfliktu
ale tse korysnyy instrument
Dorosli ukrayintsi
ale
ideal'nym
funktsional'nym
ukrayins'ki slova
Bud' laska
ukrayins'ku movu
druzhby ta solidarnosti

How do you think these letters sound? Circle the sound for each letter that you think is most likely. Then look back at the alphabet page to check.

		This sound?	Or this sound?
1	А а	a	e
2	Б б	b	ie, ye-
3	В в	v /w/	ž /ʒ/
4	Г г	h	z
5	Ґ ґ	g	y
6	Д д	d	i

		This sound?	Or this sound?
7	Е е	z	e
8	Є є	y	ie, ye-
9	Ж ж	i	ž /ʒ/
10	З з	i, yi-	z
11	И и	i, j, y-	y
12	І і	k	i

End of test. Find the answers in the text!

First words

If you want to communicate with people who are old enough to be able to read and write, make sure you both have the Google Translate app, or similar, on your **telefoni**[28]. Then you can type in what you want to say and show it to each other.

In this Star Trek like age, it is still a beautiful idea to learn some of the language to use without recourse to your **telefonu**[29]. Here are some simple **sliv**[30] to start with.

1. Hello. Pryvit. **"Pryvit"**
2. Yes. Tak. **"Tak"**
3. No. Ni. **"Nee"**
4. Please. Bud'laska. **"Bo-dlaska"**
5. Thank you. Dyakuyu. **"Jakooyoo"**

6. Sorry. Vybachte. **"we-batch-te"**
7. I don't understand. Ya ne rozumiyu. **"Ya ne rozumiyu"**
8. Show me. Pokazhy meni. **"Pokashi me-nyee"**
9. Write it here. Napyshy tse tut. **"Napushee te tut"**
10. Do you like it? Vam tse podobayet'sya? **"Vam tse podo-bayet-sya**

---

[28] telephones
[29] telephone
[30] words

11. I like it. Meni tse podobayet'sya. "**Miney tse podobayet-sya**"

12. What is it? Shcho tse. "**Shcho tse**"

13. Food. Yizha. "**Yi-zha**"

14. Drink. Pyty. "**Putee**"

15. Good. Dobre. "**Dobre**"

16. Do you want it? Vy khochete. "**Vi hodgete**"

17. I don't want it. Ya ts'oho ne khochu. "**Yatse honay hodgoo**"

18. More. Bil'she. **Blee-shu**"

19. Enough. Dostatn'o. "**Dos-tat-nyo**"

20. I don't know. Ne znayu. "**Ne znayu**"

21. Rest. Vidpochynok. "**Vidpo-chinok**"

22. I have forgotten. Ya zabuv. "**Ya zaboow**"

23. That is not necessary. Tse ne potribno. "**Tse ne potribno**"

24. Look. Podyvit'sya. "**Pody-veetsya**"

25. Here. Tut. "**Tut**"

26. Toilet. Tualet. **"Tooalet"**

27. Later. Piznishe. **"Piz-nyee-sha"**

28. Tomorrow. Zavtra. **"Zavtra"**

29. One minute. Odna khvylyna. **"Odna hwil-lina"**

30. Careful. Oberezhno. **"Oberezhno"**

31. Always. Zavzdy. **"Zavzhdy"**

32. Never. Nikoly. **"Nee-ko-le"**

33. Mine. Mij. **"Mee"**

34. Yours. Tviy. **"Twee"**

35. Come here. Khody syudy. **"Hody sudy"**

36. For sharing. Dlya obminu. **"Dla ominu"**

37. For you. Dlya tebe. **"Dla tebe"**

38. Repeat please. Povtorit', bud' laska. **"Povtoriti, bood laska"**

39. I don't speak Ukranian. YA ne rozmovlyayu ukrayins'koyu. **"Ya ne rozmov-layoo ookrayinsk-oyoo"**

40. We need Google Translate! Nam potriben Google Translate. **"Nam potriben Google Translate"**

If you could learn this set of **sliv**[31] that would be a **fantastychnyy**[32] start. It might be easy for you to make **hrupy**[33]

---

[31] Words
[32] Fantastic
[33] Groups

of 5 **sliv**[34]. Switch them around so **slova**[35] are grouped in a way that seems **lohichnym**[36] to you.

Put them on flashcards, either **fizychni**[37] ones or use a flashcard app such as Quizlet. Test yourself several times **na den'**[38], because if you are anything like me, remembering takes a lot of repetition and focus. **Chas**[39] you take is up to you, **ale**[40] I am going to add **odnu hrupu na den'**[41], and see how I get on with that. Good luck. **Udachi**.[42]

Do the learning!

Sort the phrases into groups of 5 or so words, and see if you can memorize them. Look at a phrase. Hide it. Recreate it from memory. Check if it is correct. Look at another one. See if you can remember them both. Check if they are correct. Look at another one. See if you can reproduce all three. Check if they are correct. And so on!

---

[34] Words
[35] The words
[36] Logical
[37] Physical
[38] A day
[39] The time
[40] But
[41] One group per day
[42] Good luck

Say hello

Hello Привіт Pryvit **"Pry-vit"**	Who are you? Хто ти? Khto ty? **"Khto ty"**
I'm Tom Я Том Ya Tom **"Ya Tom"**	And you? і ти? I ty? **"ee ti"**

- Pryvit. Hi.

- Pryvit. Hi

- Ya Tom. I ty? I'm Tom. And you?

- Ya Olexandr. I'm Olexandr

I learned a little **pol's'ku**[43] when I lived in Poland for 18 months, but that is it for my knowledge of Slavic languages … until now. I am using Google Translate for these, listening to the pronunciation, and repeating it several times before I write what

---

[43] Polish

I hear within the speech marks. If you feel unsure, go and have a listen.

My name	Your name
Моє ім'я	Твоє ім'я
Moye im'ya	Tvoye im'ya
"Moye ee-ya"	**"Tvoye-ee-ya"**

My name is Tom	What is your name?
Мене звати Том	як вас звати?
Mene zvaty Tom	Yak vas zvaty?
"menuh zvater Tom"	**"yak vas zvaty"**

- Ya Tom. I ty? Moye im'ya Tom. Mene zvaty Tom. Yak vas zvaty?
- Mene zvaty Mykola

Isn't it strange that to say my name, you say **moye ee-ya**, but to say my name is it changes to **menuh zvater Tom**. I suppose this is just because **anhliys'ka ta ukrayins'ka**[44] have different **typy hramatyky**[45]. As a language teacher, I think it is important to get beginners used to the sounds and meaning of some of the language before investigating the complexities of the

[44] English and Ukrainian
[45] Types of grammar

hramatyku[46]. I learned **ispans'ku**[47] for ten years before studying the grammar. That is an **ekstremal'nyy**[48] example, but we won't go into **ukrayins'ku hramatyku**[49] here and now. We just want to be welcoming and offer friendship.

Good morning доброго ранку Dobroho ranku **"dobroho ranku"**	Good afternoon доброго дня Dobroho dnya **"dobroho dnya"**
Good night Надобраніч Nadobranich **"na-dobrai-nitch"**	Goodbye до побачення do pobachennya **"do pobachennya"**

An informal way to say good bye is **па-па**. Say it like this: "pa pa". It is like saying bye-bye.

---

[46] grammar
[47] Spanish
[48] extreme
[49] Ukrainian grammar

Please	Please come in
будь ласка	будь ласка, приходьте в
Bud' laska	Bud' laska, prykhot'te v
"bo-dlaska"	**"bo-dlaska, prehote"**

As I have never met Ukranian people before, I am trying to read about the nation **v interneti**[50]. Some of it might be true!

Ya chytav[51], that Ukrainians like to dress smart, particularly **zhinky**[52]. It says men are expected to be chivalrous, opening doors, pulling out chairs and paying **v restoranakh**[53]. **Ukrayins'ka babusya**,[54] or granny is small, tough and wears a headscarf. The national dish is borscht, a beet soup with lots of variety. The cuisine is based on plentiful grain and vegetables such as potato, cabbage, mushroom and beetroot.

This quote is from theculturetrip.com, 16th July, 2018.

"Ukrainians are very friendly and welcoming. They love **velyki hrupy**[55] and gatherings, always help each other and consider all people around them to be their best **druzyamy**[56]."

---

[50] On the internet
[51] I read
[52] The women
[53] In restaurants
[54] The Ukrainian granny
[55] Large groups
[56] Friends

Guess Test Two

Look at these words that were embedded in the text in the SAY HELLO section. Can you guess what any of them mean?

pol's'ku

anhliys'ka ta ukrayins'ka

typy hramatyky

hramatyku

ispans'ku

ekstremal'nyy

ukrayins'ku hramatyku

v Interneti

Ya chytav

Zhinky

u restoranakh

Ukrayins'ka babusya

velyki hrupy

druzyamy

Record yourself speaking

Record yourself and listen back. Save the file.

Good morning	Dobroho ranku
Hi	Pryvit
I'm Tom	Ya Tom
And you?	I ty?
What are you called?	Yak vas zvaty?
My name is Mick	Mene zvaty Mick

How do you think these letters sound? Circle the sound for each letter that you think is most likely. Then look back at the alphabet page to check.

		This sound?	Or this sound?
13	Ï ï	i, yi-	E
14	Й й	i, j, y-	ie, ye-
15	К к	k	ž /ʒ/
16	Л л	o	L
17	М м	p	M
18	Н н	r	N

End of test.

Welcome to our home

This is our home	You are welcome
це наш дім	ласкаво просимо
Tse nash dim	Laskavo prosymo
"tse nash deem"	**"laskavo prosymo"**
Please sit down	Would you like a drink?
Будь ласка, сідайте	хочете випити?
Bud' laska, sidayte	Khochete vypyty?
"bo-dlaska, see-ye-day-te"	**"hotche-te vi-pe-te"**

Read it out loud, altogether.

1. **"Tse nash deem. Laskavo prosymo. Bo-dlasksa, seeyedayte. Hotchete vipete?"**

   Tse nash dim. Laskavo prosymo. Bud' laska, sidayte. Khochete vypyty?

As a language teacher, I encourage **studentiv praktykuvaty**[57] memorizing set pieces during lessons and for homework. My parents used to do this with **moyimy bratamy**[58] and me at the dinner **stolom**[59] … we can all ask for a hankerchief in German! **V**

---

[57] Students to practice
[58] My brothers
[59] table

dytynstvi my[60] memorized sentences with lots of repetition, along with competition to prove who was the most intelligent and the quickest. It was **veselo**[61]!

To memorize a set piece like the one here, **ya rekomenduyu**[62] a combination of presence, effort and demonstration (otherwise known as showing off!) For presence, make sure you have the language to hand, written down in **ukrayins'koyu ta anhliys'koyu**[63], and in your back pocket whenever it isn't in front of your eyes. For effort do the look, test, check **metodu**[64] of learning. **Demonstratsiya prosta**[65]. **Znaydy druha**[66] and tell them what you have learned. Even better, teach it to them too.

You must be tired	This is your bedroom
ти напевне стомився	Це твоя спальня
ty napevne stomyvsya	Tse tvoya spal'nya
"te napevne stom-wi-sia"	**"tse tvoya spal-nya"**

---

[60] As children we
[61] fun
[62] I recommend
[63] Ukrainian and English
[64] method
[65] Demonstration is easy
[66] Find a friend

Here are towels for you ось рушники для вас Os' rushnyky dlya vas **"os roosh-nicki dlya vas"**	For laundry Для прання Dlya prannya **"dlya prannya"**
This is the wifi code Це код Wi-Fi Tse kod Wi-Fi **"tse code Wi-Fi"**	These are for you Це для вас Tse dlya vas **"tse deeya vas"**

Here are some tips from the hospitality industry. Let your guests know it is a pleasure for you to be their host. Thank them, tell them they are welcome, and ask them if you can get them anything, as they might be too shy to ask for themselves.

I am happy to help you Я радий вам допомогти YA radyy vam dopomohty **"YA rady vam dopomohty"**	Thank you Дякую Dyakuyu **"jakooyoo"**
Welcome ласкаво просимо Laskavo prosymo **"laskavo prosimo"**	Can I get you anything? можу я тобі щось принести? Mozhu ya tobi shchos' prynesty? **"moshoo ya to-beesh chos prinisty"**

Do the learning

Look back and note down the following Ukrainian words and phrases. Then choose five to memorize. Even if you can't remember them later, it will be easier the next time you try.

1. This is our home

2. You are welcome

3. Please sit down

4. Would you like a drink?

5. You must be tired

6. This is your bedroom

7. Here are towels for you

8. For laundry

9. This is the wifi code

10. These are for you

11. I am happy to help you

12. Thank you

13. Welcome

14. Can I get you anything?

Guess Test Three

Look at these words that were embedded in the text in the WELCOME TO OUR HOME section. Can you guess what any of them mean? Some are more difficult than others!

Studentiv

Praktykuvaty

moyimy bratamy

stolom

U dytynstvi

Ya rekomenduyu

ukrayins'koyu

ta

anhliys'koyu

metodu

Demonstratsiya prosta

Znaydy druha

Record yourself speaking

Record yourself and listen back. Save the file.

Welcome	Laskavo prosymo
This is our home	Tse nash dim
Would you like a drink?	Khochete vypyty?
Yes please	Tak bud'laska.
I like it	Meni tse podobayet'sya
This is for you	Tse dlya tebe
Thank you	Dyakuyu
This is your bedroom	Tse tvoya spal'nya

How do you think these letters sound? Circle the sound for each letter that you think is most likely. Then look back at the alphabet page to check.

		This sound?	Or this sound?
19	O o	o	F
20	П п	kh	P
21	P p	r	Ts
22	C c	ch	S
23	T т	t	Sh

End of test.

Families

My mother	My father
моя мати	мій батько
moya maty	miy bat'ko
"moya maty"	**"me batchko"**

My children	My friend
мої діти	мій друг
moyi dity	miy druh
"moyi dyiti"	**"mee drooer"**

When I was 12 I went to Germany on a town exchange trip. I stayed with a wonderful family who are still my friends, and they are still in my life now, several decades after we first met.

I stayed with my German **druha**[67], Andrea, several times. **Yiyi bat'ky**[68] were both kind and engaging. Brunhilde, **maty**[69] (now **babusya**[70]) is the quieter of the couple because she speaks less **anhliys'koyu**[71]. She was almost always busy, and if it was

---

[67] friend
[68] Her parents
[69] The mother
[70] grandmother
[71] English

something **vesele**[72], like cooking or tending to **kuramy**[73], she would beckon me and invite me to join in.

Gunter, **bat'ko**[74] (now grandfather) was confident to use the minimal English he had to talk to me at every opportunity. He would say the same things **znovu i znovu**[75]. Some of his favourite things to say were **moya anhliys'ka ideal'na**[76], your German is perfect, you are an ambassador for England ... as well as telling me that he could eat a banana sideways because his mouth is so wide! Gunter and Brunhilde didn't ask me too many questions, **ale**[77] they succeeded in making me feel like I was part of the **sim'yi**.[78]

If you are welcoming **ukrayintsiv**[79] people **u svoyemu domi**[80] or community, you will find your own way to do it. Fleeing from war is very different to a cultural exchange trip. The people you meet will probably need **kompaniya**[81] of other Ukranian people rather than having extended conversations across **movnyy bar''yer**[82].

---

[72] fun
[73] The chickens
[74] The father
[75] Over and over again
[76] My English is perfect
[77] but
[78] family
[79] Ukrainian
[80] Into your home
[81] The company
[82] A language barrier

That is why I think Gunter and Brunhilde are a good model. They were unintrusive, they gave me space to rest, they were happy for me talk to other English speakers and they were open and welcoming when I was ready to engage.

Ukranian people will want to be part of Ukranian communities. However, you are at home. You know how things work here, and your support is important. You can enable those connections. You can help people charge their devices, maintain contact with loved ones and access services. Whether you help with a kind **slovom**[83] or with space **u vashomu domi**[84], you are making a difference. Keep love in your **sertsi**,[85] and know that it is difficult and you are doing your best.

In this section we are exploring and studying some **slova**[86] related to family. Later on I will look at language related to communication, accessing services, house rules and so on. This is not a linear **kurs**[87]. If you would like to skip ahead of course you can. Every section of this book is for **absolyutnykh**[88] beginners so it doesn't matter if you want to prioritise another section.

---

[83] word
[84] In your home
[85] heart
[86] words
[87] course
[88] absolute

Family	Parents
сім'ї	батьків
sim'yi	bat'kiv
"sim-yi"	**"bat-kiy"**

Brothers	Sisters
брати	сестри
braty	sestry
"braty"	**"sistry"**

Sons	Daughters
синів	дочок
syniv	dochok
"sinew"	**"door-chok"**

Grandfather	Grandmother
дідусь	бабуся
didus'	babusya
"deer-doois"	**"bor-boo-isa"**

Slova[89] like **sim'ya, brat i dochka**[90] are nouns. You might have noticed (you might not have noticed) that the endings of nouns change quite a lot. **Ukrayina**[91] is a noun. Here are some examples of how it changes.

---

[89] Words
[90] Famiy, brother and daughter
[91] Ukraine

1. Ukraine is a large country.

   Україна велика країна.

   Ukrayina velyka krayina.

2. Kyiv is the capital of Ukraine.

   Київ є столицею україни.

   Kyyiv ye stolytseyu **Ukrayiny.**

3. You must visit Ukraine.

   Ви повинні відвідати Україну.

   Vy povynni vidvidaty **Ukrayinu.**

Moya meta[92] here is to learn a few words in Ukranian so that I can welcome people who might come into my community **z Ukrayiny.**[93] **Ya novachok**[94], so I am going to try to learn as much as possible as fast as possible. **Yak dytyna**[95] who is learning to speak for the first time, I am aiming for communication.

As I make progress, I might become interested in the rules that govern the correct endings for the nouns, but that will be later … much later!

Brother can be **brat, brata, bratovi, bratom, brati, brate.**

Sister can be **sestra, sestry, sestru, sestroyu, sestri, sestro.**

---

[92] My aim
[93] From Ukraine
[94] I'm a beginner
[95] Like a baby

If I am talking about **brativ i sester**[96] in the plural there are even more words, and getting them right will take too much bandwidth in the brain of a beginner **yak ya**[97].

At this point therefore, I don't want to slow or stall my progress by paying attention to something that I think is too difficult for me to grasp. **Ya znayu**[98] that there are differences, and for now, that is enough. Try to learn some key **sliv**[99]. When you meet Ukranian people, try to use some of your key **sliv i fraz**[100]. Here is a convenient list of **rodynnykh sliv**[101].

Family	Сім'я	Sim'ya
Mother and father	Мати та батько	Maty ta bat'ko
Brother and sister	Брат і сестра	Brat i sestra
Son and daughter	Син і дочка	Syn i dochka
Grandmother	бабуся	Babusya
Grandfather	Дідусь	Didus'
Children	Діти	Dity
Friend	Друг	Druh
Love	Любов	Lyubov

---

[96] Brothers and sisters
[97] Like me
[98] I know
[99] Words
[100] Words and phrases. Actually, when you meet Ukrainian people, I think it will be best to be attentive to their needs, rather than to have the intention of using this word or that. I hope that makes sense.
[101] Family words

Sim'ya[102] is an important **tema**[103] for humans. The hard **pravda**[104] is that **sim'yi z Ukrayiny**[105] have been separated, as **dorosli**[106] men are required to stay and **mil'yoni zhinok**[107] are leaving in search of safety for themselves **ta svoyikh ditey**[108].

I think **simeyni slova**[109] are important for a couple of reasons.

- If members of your **rodyny**[110] ever come to **vas dodomu**[111], they will be coming into the temporary home of any **bizhentsiv**[112] you are hosting. It might be good **manery**[113] to present them.

- People may have travelled and found places to stay in **simeynykh hrupakh**[114]. Mothers and their **dity**[115] may have **rodychiv ta druziv**[116] at an accessible **vidstani**[117], perhaps also taking refuge in your town or city. If so, a

---

[102] Family
[103] topic
[104] Truth
[105] Families from Ukraine
[106] adult
[107] Millions of women
[108] And their children
[109] Family words
[110] Family – yes! A completely different word!
[111] Your house
[112] refugees
[113] manners
[114] Family groups
[115] children
[116] Relatives and friends
[117] distance

person might like help to maintain **kontakt, ya ne znayu**[118].

I think we just need to remain aware, and listen to people. I think we need to pay attention **na slova** (to words), voice and body language, and try to do our best.

This is my father це мій батько Tse miy bat'ko **"tse mee batko"**	This is my brother це мій брат Tse miy brat **"tse mee brat"**
This is my son це мій син Tse miy syn **"tse mee sin"**	This is my mother Це моя мама Tse moya mama **"tse moya mama"**
This is my sister це моя сестра Tse moya sestra **"tse moya sestra"**	This is my daughter це моя дочка Tse moya dochka **"tse moya dutch-ka"**
She is beautiful вона прекрасна Vona prekrasna **"vona prekrasna"**	Where is she? де вона De vona? **"de vona"**

---

[118] Contact, I don't know.

Guess Test Four

Look at these words that were embedded in the text
in the FAMILIES section. It's a big section.

Make your guesses!

yiyi bat'ky

anhliys'koyu

znovu i znovu

sim'yi

kompaniya

movnyy bar''yer

moya meta

yak dytyna

ya znayu

mil'yoni zhinok

vas dodomu

simeynykh hrupakh

na slova

How do you think these letters sound? Circle the
sound for each letter that you think is most likely.
Then look back at the alphabet page to check.

		This sound?	Or this sound?
24	У у	u	Ts
25	Ф ф	ch	F
26	Х х	sh	Kh

Record yourself speaking

Record yourself and listen back. Save the file.

This is my mother	Tse miy mat'ko
Hello What are you called?	Pryvit Yak vas zvaty?
I'm called Mary What are you called?	Mene zvaty Mary Yak vas zvaty?
I'm called Kateryna This is my sister	Mene zvaty Kateryna Tse moya sestra
She is beautiful Where is she?	Vona prekrasna De vona?
Here in England	Tut, v Anhliyi

End of test.

House rules part one

It is a good idea to talk about house rules if you have a stranger coming to stay. If you tell your guest to make themselves at home, this might be welcoming **ale**[119] it might also be bewildering. House rules are a good **ideyeyu**[120] for everyone involved. I hope you can **adaptuvaty**[121] the suggestions I make to suit your situation.

I am coming from a position of personal ignorance, never having hosted a refugee. I have read other people's testimonies, and I hope that some of what I offer can be useful to you.

At the door

Come in	Welcome
увійдіть	Ласкаво просимо
Uviydit'	Laskavo prosymo
"uvi-yit"	**"Laskavo prosymo"**

Lock the door	Put your shoes here
Замкнути двері	Поставте туфлі сюди
Zamknuty dveri	Postavte tufli syudy
"zamknuty dvi-ree"	**"postavte tufi surdee"**

---

[119] but
[120] idea
[121] adapt

In the kitchen

This cupboard is for you Ця шафа для вас Tsya shafa dlya vas **"tsa shafa dear vas"**	This shelf is for you Ця полиця для вас Tsya polytsya dlya vas **"tsa politcia dear vas"**
You can cook Можна готувати Mozhna hotuvaty **"mozhna hotuvaty"**	You can use these Ви можете використовувати ці Vy mozhete vykorystovuvaty tsi **"ve mozhete vekory- stovu-vaty tsi"**
Wash your dishes помий посуд Pomyy posud **"pomy posud"**	Put rubbish here кладіть сюди сміття Kladit' syudy smittya **"kladit syudy smitya"**
This can be recycled це можна переробити Tse mozhna pererobyty **"tse mozhna pererobiti"**	This is compost Це компост Tse kompost **"Tse kompost"**

Can is a recurrent word. Може. **Mozhe**. I am enjoying some of the sounds of Ukranian, such as the zh. It is like sh but with a z. I can is я можу, **ya mozhu**. You can is ти можеш. **Ty mozhesh.**

Times and routines

I go to sleep at ten	I wake up at six
Я лягаю спати о десятій	Я прокидаюся о шостій
Ya lyahayu spaty o desyatiy	Ya prokydayusya o shostiy
"ya lyahayu spaty o desyeti"	**"Ya proke-dayusu o shoisti"**
Be quiet when I am asleep	I cook at half past six
Тихо, коли я сплю	Готую о пів на шосту
Tykho, koly ya splyu	Hotuyu o piv na shostu
"Tiho koly ya spew"	**"Hotuyu o piv na shostu"**
I go out at seven	I come home at six
Я виходжу о сьомій	Приходжу додому о шостій
Ya vyhodzhu o s'omiy	Prykhodzhu dodomu o shostiy
"ya vhodzhu o syomy"	**"pryhodzhu dodomu o shoisty"**

I don't know = Не знаю, Ne znayu.

Ya ne znayu your routine. Here is a big old **kolektsiya** of clock times that you might like to try to chant. With the Ukranian sounds that are so unfamiliar to **anhlomovnykh**[122], it's going to

---

[122] English speakers

be a real tongue twister! From what I gather, in Ukranian you say something like this: first hour, fifteen minutes; or second hour, thirty minutes. Let's do it! At the very least, I am getting an idea of the sounds. In the table we have English, the Roman alphabet transliteration, and how I hear it … that is in the speech marks.

First hour	Persha hodyna
"persha hodinna"	
Second hour	Druha hodyna
"drooha hodinna"	
Third hour	Tretya hodyna
"tretya hodinna"	
Forth hour	Chetverta hodyna
"chetwerta hodinna"	
Fifth hour	P'yata hodyna
"pyata hodinna"	
Sixth hour	Shosta hodyna
"shosta hodinna"	
Seventh hour	S'oma hodyna
"syoma hodinna"	
Eighth hour	Vos'ma hodyna
"voisma hodinna"	
Nineth hour	Dev'yata hodyna
"dev'yata hodinna"	

Tenth hour	Desyata hodyna
"desyata hodinna"	
Eleventh hour	Odynadtsyata hodyna
"odynait-syita hodinna"	
Twelfth hour	Dvanadtsyata hodyna
"dva-nait-syita hodinna"	

All this talk of hot dinners (**hodinna**) is making me hungry! I have my lunch at "**dva-nait-syita hodinna**" and now it is 11:40. Let's have a look at the minutes.

Five minutes	P'yat' khvylyn
"pyet hoolin"	
Ten minutes	Desyat' khvylyn
"day-syit hoolin"	
Fifteen minutes	P'yatnadtsyat' khvylyn
"Piyet-naisit hoolin"	
Twenty minutes	Dvadtsyat' khvylyn
"dvai-sitch hoolin"	
Twenty five minutes	dvadtsyat' p'yat' khvylyn
"dvai-sitch pyet hoolin"	
Thirty minutes	trydtsyat' khvylyn
"trit-sitch hoolin"	

Thirty five minutes	Trydtsyat' p'yat' khvylyn
"trit-sitch pyet hoolin"	
Forty minutes	Sorok khvylyn
"sorok hoolin"	
Forty five minutes	Sorok p'yat' khvylyn
"sorok pyet hoolin"	
Fifty minutes	P'yatdesyat khvylyn
"pyet-desyat hoolin"	
Fifty five minutes	p'yatdesyat p'yat' khvylyn
"pyet-desyat pyet hoolin"	

Now you can make any **chas**[123] you like. 11:40 is eleventh hour: "odynait-syita hodinna"; forty minutes: "sorok pyet hoolin". What time do you have dinner? If you have the patience, it is a great exercise to count through the hours in five minute **intervalamy**[124]. In language classes that is called a drill, and they are a little bit out of **mody**[125]. They work **dobre**[126], though. Drills help you learn the vocabulary and give you confidence, and can be a good part of your language learning **stratehiyi**[127].

---

[123] time
[124] intervals
[125] fashion
[126] well
[127] strategy

Private space/ shared space

If someone is coming to stay with you they will need their own space and so will you. Refugees come with **stresom i shokom**[128], and they usually need somewhere safe, dry and quiet to make **kontakt**[129] with their **blyz'kymy**[130].

Once you have made sure their immediate **fizychni**[131] needs are met and they are able to charge **svoyi telefony**[132], they will probably want to shut the door.

Being a host to a stranger in need may take a lot of **emotsiynoyi enerhiyi**[133] from you, and you will need your space, alone or with your own **blyz'kymy**[134]. Here are some things you might like to say.

This room is mine	This is private
ця кімната моя	це приватне
tsya kimnata moya	Tse pryvatne
"tsya kimnata moya"	**"tse privatne"**

---

[128] Stress and shock
[129] contact
[130] Loved ones
[131] physical
[132] Their telephones
[133] Emotional energy
[134] Loved ones

This room is yours ця кімната твоя Tsya kimnata tvoya **"tsya kimnata tvoya"**	Don't go in there Не заходь туди Ne zakhod' tudy **"ne zahod tudy"**
This is my children's room Це моя дитяча кімната Tse moya dytyacha kimnata **"tse moya dichersha** **kimnata"**	You can sit here with us ти можеш сидіти тут з нами Ty mozhesh sydity tut z namy **"ti mozhesh sidyiti tut** **znamy"**

I like **slova**[135] for child and children. Let's have a look at a few of them. Dytyna is child, and dity is children. My child is moya dytyna, and my children is moyi dity. One way of saying your child is vasha dytyna, and your children is vashi dity. Another way of saying your child is tvoya dytyna, and your children, tvoyi dity.

I am finding out that there is a lot of complexity in Ukranian. I was expecting it, and I can cope because **ya ne perfektsionist**[136]!

I have just found one more useful word. Ok is harazd, pronounced "harad". Learn the word harazd.

---

[135] The words
[136] I'm not a perfectionist

Guess Test Five

Look at these words that were embedded in the text in HOUSE RULES PART ONE. Can you guess what they mean? Check your answers in the text if you want to.

Ideyeyu

Adaptuvaty

Mozhe

YA ne znayu

Intervalamy

Mody

Dobre

Stratehiya

Stresom i shokom

Kontakt

Blyz'kymy

Svoyi telefony

Emotsiynoyi enerhiyi

Ya ne perfektsionist

Record yourself speaking

Record yourself and listen back. Save the file.

Come in	Uviydit'
Put your shoes here	Postavte tufli syudy
This cupboard is for you	Tsya shafa dlya vas
Thank you	Dyakuyu
You can cook	Mozhna hotuvaty
Put rubbish here	Pokladit' syudy smittya
Ok	Harazd
Good night	Nadobranich
Good night	Nadobranich

How do you think these letters sound? Circle the sound for each letter that you think is most likely. Then look back at the alphabet page to check.

		This sound?	Or this sound?
30	Щ щ	shch	kh
32	Ю ю	ch	iu, yu-
33	Я я	sh	ia, ya-

End of test.

House rules part two

Housework

One of the things I have read in accounts of refugees is that they often have the feeling that life is in limbo. Doing simple tasks, together or alone, can help make **chas**[137] feel more purposeful. So you might like to offer little **roboty**[138] to a person.

As part of the house rules you might also want or need to ask a person to clean up after themselves. Here are a few phrases. The aim is to get used to a little bit **do movy**[139].

This is the vacuum cleaner	This is how it works
Це пилосос	Ось як це працює
Tse pylosos	Os' yak tse pratsyuye
"tse pilosos"	**"os yak tse pratsuye"**

You can clean your room	Can you help me?
Ви можете прибрати свою кімнату	можеш допомогти мені
Vy mozhete prybraty svoyu kimnatu ...**"Vy mozhete prybraty svoyu kimnatu"**	Mozhesh dopomohty meni **"mozhesh dopomohty menyi"**

---

[137] time
[138] jobs
[139] Of the language

The bathroom

Kievtourguide.com writes this (12 November 2019): "It might come as a surprise to many travellers to Ukraine that flushing **tualetnyy papir**[140] in Ukraine is **absolyutno**[141] no-no! Ukraine is not unique here, there are several Western European countries where flushing paper down the toilet is not the correct thing to do."

This means that you might need to tell your **ukrayins'kym hostyam**[142] what can and cannot be flushed down the toilet **u vashomu domi!**[143] **Delikatna rozmova**[144] that can be done easily with **sliv yak tak**[145], here, not this, this goes here.

This yes	This no
це так	це ні
Tse tak	Tse ni
"tse tak"	"tsay nee"

---

[140] Toilet paper
[141] An absolute
[142] Ukrainian guests
[143] In your home
[144] A delicate conversation
[145] Words like yes

This in the toilet	This in the bin
Це в туалеті	це в кошику
Tse v tualeti	Tse v koshyku
"tse twal-yet-yi"	**"tse v kosyku"**

You might like to create a bathroom picture dictionary. This could be useful, and will definitely help you to learn and use some of the vocabulary. Here are some words you could include.

Bathroom	Ванна кімната	Vanna kimnata
Toilet	туалет	Tualet
Toilet paper	туалетний папір	Tualetnyy papir
Bin	смітник	Smitnyk
Sink	раковина	Rakovyna "takovyna"
Hot water	гаряча вода	Haryacha voda
Cold water	холодна вода	kholodna voda "holodna voda"
Toothpaste	зубна паста	Zubna pasta
Toothbrush	зубна щітка	Zubna shchitka
Cupboard	шафа	Shafa
Mirror	Дзеркало	Dzerkalo
Shelf	полиця	Polytsya
Shower	душ	Dush
Towel	Рушник	Rushnyk

In my house we have **odna vanna kimnata**[146]. It has **dush**[147], **rakovyna**[148], a couple of **shaf**[149] and a mirror. It is the place where I go **v tualet**[150], wash, **chyshchu zuby**[151] and put on my make-up.

If I had **hosti**[152] I would want them to leave **vannu kimnatu**[153] clean and dry. I would want clean **rushnyky**[154] hung up on the towel rail or on another radiator. I would want **brudny rushnyky**[155] to be put in the laundry basket, or in the washing machine if there was a full load to go in. I don't have many **hostey**[156] come to stay.

I read on the site, borgenproject.org (24 March, 2017), that tap **voda**[157] in the southern regions of Ukraine is not safe to drink. So one more thing you might like to tell your **hostyu**[158] is if it is safe to drink your tap **vodu**[159].

---

[146] One bathroom
[147] A shower
[148] A sink
[149] cupboards
[150] To the toilet
[151] Brush my teeth
[152] guests
[153] The bathroom
[154] towels
[155] Dirty towels
[156] guests
[157] water
[158] guest
[159] water

Guess Test Six

Look at these words that were embedded in the text in HOUSE RULES PART TWO. Try to guess what they mean, and check your answers in the text.

Chas

Roboty

Do movy

Tualetnyy papir

Absolyutno

Ukrayins'kym hostyam

U vashomu domi

Delikatna rozmovathat

Sliv yak tak

Odna vanna kimnata

Dush

Rakovyna

Hosti

Voda

Record yourself speaking

Record yourself and listen back. Save the file.

Can you help me please?	Mozhesh meni dopomohty bud'laska
This is the vacuum cleaner	Tse pylosos
Good. Thank you	Dobre. Dyakuyu

Match the threes

The task here is to match the words in the Ukrainian alphabet, the transcriptions in our alphabet and with the English words. Three per group. A real puzzle!

туалет	Zubna pasta
смітник	Tualet
зубна паста	Smitnyk
шафа	Rushnyk
душ	Shafa
Рушник	Dush

bin, cupboard, shower, toilet, toothpaste, towel

End of test.

About communication

The goal of **movy**[160] is to communicate. The goal of this **bukletu**[161] is to get started with the sounds, the vocabulary, the differences **v hramatytsi**[162], and above all, with the confidence to have a go. The top **instrumentom**[163] for those who can write will be an app such as Google Translate. **Tse ne ideal'no, ale duzhe dobre**[164].

Speak slowly	Say that again
говори повільно	скажи це ще раз
Hovory povil'no	Skazhy tse shche raz
"hovory povilno"	**"skazhy tse sh-che raz"**
Show me	Teach me
Покажи мені	навчи мене
Pokazhy meni	Navchy mene
"pokazhy menyi"	**"navche menay"**

My mozhemo[165] communicate a massive amount of meaning **bez sliv**[166], through showing and acting. Communicating with limited

---

[160] language
[161] booklet
[162] In the grammar
[163] tool
[164] It isn't perfect, but it is very good
[165] We can
[166] Without words

movoyu[167] is an act of creativity, and can be very satisfying. Combine a great translation app, and a willingness to learn, and you have a winning **kombinatsiya**.[168]

I don't understand	Do you understand?
я не розумію	Ти розумієш
Ya ne rozumiyu	Ty rozumiyesh
"ya ne rozumiyu"	**"ti rozumiyesh"**

Is it wrong?	I am sorry
Чи це неправильно	Вибачте
Chy tse nepravyl'no	Vybachte
"chy tse nepravylno"	**"wibatch-te"**

Duolingo is another brilliant place for you to learn a little more Ukranian. There is a reason it is such **populyarnyy dodatok**[169]. It is easy to access and it is a pleasant way to spend **trokhy chasu**[170] with your new **movoyu**[171]. If you haven't already installed it as one of your favourites, make sure you download it next **razu**[172] you are **na svoyemu telefoni.**[173]

---

[167] language
[168] combination
[169] A popular app
[170] A little time
[171] language
[172] time
[173] On your telephone

You speak too fast Ви говорите занадто швидко Vy hovoryte zanadto shvydko **"wi hovorite zanadto shwidko"**	I speak too fast Я говорю занадто швидко YA hovoryu zanadto shvydko **"ya hovoru zanadto shwidko"**
Repeat after me повторюй за мною Povtoryuy za mnoyu **"Povtory za moyu"**	Little by little мало-помалу Malo-pomalu **"malo po malo"**

When you start trying to communicate with a real human being, it will inevitably be quite different to playing **v dodatku**[174] or reading this book. You will need to be honest (always the best **polityka**[175]). Say when you don't **rozumiyesh**[176]. If your message is important, don't give up if you don't get it across **pershoho razu**.[177]

---

[174] On an app
[175] policy
[176] understand
[177] The first time

I like this word Мені подобається це слово Meni podobayet'sya tse slovo **"meni podo-bite-se tse slovo"**	What is this in Ukranian? як це українською Yak tse ukrayins'koyu **"Yak tse oo-kray-ins-koyu"**
Be patient Будьте терплячі Bud'te terplyachi **"bud-te terplechi"**	It is complicated Це складно Tse skladno **"tse skladno"**

When we speak, **nashi aktsenty**[178] will probably be horrible, and so will **nasha hramatyka**[179]. If someone is being kind enough to try to teach you, have a go at repeating what they are saying.

I like your accent Мені подобається твій акцент Meni podobayet'sya tviy aktsent **"meni podo-bay-sa tvi akt-sent"**	You speak well ти добре говориш Ty dobre hovorysh **"ti dob-re ho-worish"**

---

[178] Our accents
[179] Our grammar

How do you say this?	Tell me again
як ти це кажеш?	Розкажи мені знову
Yak ty tse kazhesh?	Rozkazhy meni znovu
"yak ti tse kazhesh"	**"rozkazhy menyi znovu"**

Yak novachok[180] though, it will be so difficult. If **vasha hramatyka**[181] and **aktsent**[182] are all wrong, **ale lyudyna vas rozumiye**[183], take that as a win. So you said something like my friend, and it should have been my friend-u, or my friend-ia ... **Ya ne znayu**[184]! In my book, beginners are winners if they get the dart somewhere on the dart board. You don't have to hit the bullseye!

---

[180] As a beginner
[181] Your grammar
[182] accent
[183] But the person understands you
[184] I don't know

Guess Test Seven

Look at these words that were embedded in the text in ABOUT COMMUNICATION. Try to guess what they mean, and check your answers in the text.

Bukletu

Hramatytsi

Tse ne ideal'no

Ale duzhe dobre

Bez sliv

Kombinatsiya

Populyarnyy dodatok

Na svoyemu telefoni

Polityka

Rozumiyesh

Aktsenty

Novachok

Lyudyna vas rozumiye

YA ne znayu

Record yourself speaking

Record yourself and listen back. Save the file.

What is this in Ukranian?	Yak tse ykrayins'koyu?
Food	Yizha
You speak too fast Say that again	Vy hovoryte zanadto shvydko Skazhy tse shche raz
Food You speak well	Yizha Ty dobre hovorysh
Thank you	Dyakuyu

How do you think these letters sound? Circle the sound for each letter that you think is most likely. Then look back at the alphabet page to check.

		This sound?	Or this sound?
9	Ж ж	ž /ʒ/	v
11	И и	y	n
16	Л л	l	f
20	П п	r	p
27	Ц ц	yu	ts
29	Ш ш	ch	sh
33	Я я	b	ia, ya-

Match the threes

Match the words in the Ukrainian alphabet, the transcriptions in our alphabet and the English words. Three per group. A real puzzle!

мало-помалу	Rozkazhy meni znovu
як ти це кажеш?	Malo-pomalu
Розкажи мені знову	Yak ty tse kazhesh?

little by little, tell me again, how do you say this?

I would like to look at the more exotic letters. Copy them, and use them in the example words: віжон.

Ж ж	Ф ф	Ю ю	Я я
ž /ʒ/ si in vision	f f in fox	iu, yu- you in you	ia, ya- ya in yam

End of test.

Basic needs

Meals

I tend to eat breakfast at **s'oma hodyna**[185], lunch at **dvanadtsyata hodyna**[186], and my evening meal at about **shosta hodyna**[187]. I have tea and coffee throughout the day too. Let's find out what that vocabulary is in Ukranian.

Breakfast	Lunch
сніданок	обід
Snidanok	Obid
"snee-danok"	**"obeed"**

Evening meal	Tea and coffee
вечеря	чай і кава
Vercherya	Chay i kava
"wer-cher-ria"	**"Chay i kawa"**

Na snidanok[188] I usually have a cup **chayu**[189] and a bowl of oats soaked in soya **molosti**[190]. In general, Ukrainians eat bread and

---

[185] Seventh hour
[186] Twelfth hour
[187] Sixth hour
[188] For breakfast
[189] Of tea
[190] milk

butter, **do chayu chy kawy**[191], or pastries. Or they might have steamed buckwheat, barley or millet **z molokom**[192].

Na obid[193] I usually have a sandwich ... maybe fried egg or perhaps cheese **salat**[194]. I often have a piece of **fruktiv**[195] too, and maybe **paketyk chipsiv**[196].

According to the website, foodbycountry.com, the main meal in Ukraine is eaten around mid-afternoon and usually consists **z supu**[197] and a dish with meat or poultry.

For my **vecheri**[198] tonight I had pasta. Yesterday I made a leek and potato dish. I often have **vehetarians'kyy hamburher i chipsy z brokkoli**[199] or sweetcorn. I have most variety in my evening meal, and it is my main meal of the day.

Foodbycountry.com tells me that it is considered impolite to put your elbows on the table. It says, "Ukrainians may eat everything on their plates. When they are visiting, Ukrainians may ask for second helpings to show appreciation for the food. Hosts often

---

[191] With tea or coffee
[192] With milk
[193] For lunch
[194] salad
[195] fruit
[196] A packet of crisps
[197] Of soup
[198] Evening meal
[199] A vegetarian burger and chips with broccoli

give guests a loaf of bread with salt on top, **tradytsiya**[200] that dates back many centuries. Bread and salt were once considered necessary **inhrediyentamy**[201] for health. The bread represents hospitality and the salt represents **druzhbu**[202]."

If you invite **ukrayintsiv**[203] to eat and drink with you, you might like to make **tost**[204]. Here are a couple of suggestions for raising your glasses.

To our meeting	To friends
за зустріч	для друзів
Za zustrich	Dlya druziv
"za zustrich"	**"dla druziw"**

We all hope that **viyna v Ukrayini**[205] will be over as soon as possible, perhaps before I finish writing this book, or before you finish reading it. As soon as possible.

We all hope that Ukrainian people will be able to return to their **domivok**[206] and rebuild their lives in prosperity and peace. I hope that we can learn some of this **prekrasnu movu**[207], and use it **yak**

---

[200] A tradition
[201] ingredients
[202] friendship
[203] Ukrainians
[204] A toast
[205] War in Ukraine
[206] homes
[207] Beautiful language

turysty[208] visiting this amazing **krayinu**[209]. I hope we can be welcomed **yak hosti**[210] of Ukrainian people, and raise these **tosti**[211] at their tables. To peace. **Za myr.**[212]

....

Za myr.

....

---

[208] As tourists
[209] country
[210] As guests
[211] toasts
[212] To peace

Guess Test Eight

Look at these words that were embedded in the text in MEALS. Try to guess what they mean, and check your answers in the text.

Shosta hodyna

Chayu ta kawy

Z molokom

Salat

Frukty

Paketyk chipsiv

Sup

Vehetarians'kyy hamburher

Chipsy z brokkoli

Inhrediyentamy

Druzhbu

Yak turysty

Krayinu

Yak hosti

Record yourself speaking

Record yourself and listen back. Save the file.

Breakfast	Snidanok
I don't understand	Ya ne rozumiyu
Show me	Pokazhy meni
Tea and coffee	Chay i kava
Do you like it?	Vam tse podobayet'sya?
I like it, yes	Meni tse podobayet'sya, tak
Thank you	Dyakuyu

How do you think these letters sound? Circle the sound for each letter that you think is most likely. Then look back at the alphabet page to check.

		This sound?	Or this sound?
1	A a	a	e
2	Б б	v	b
10	З з	e	z
12	I i	i	l
13	Ї ї	i, yi-	y
15	K к	r	k
17	M м	sh	m
19	O o	a	o
20	П п	p	r

Match the threes

Match the words in the Ukrainian alphabet, the transcriptions in our alphabet and the English words. Three per group. A real puzzle!

снiданок	Obid
обiд	Vercherya
вечеря	Snidanok

breakfast, lunch and evening meal

I would like to look at some of the fricative sounds. Copy them, and use them in the example words.

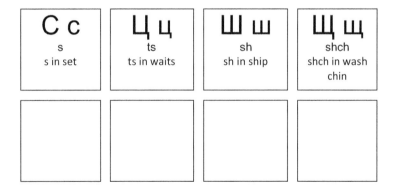

С с	Ц ц	Ш ш	Щ щ
s	ts	sh	shch
s in set	ts in waits	sh in ship	shch in wash chin

End of test.

Basic needs: Getting about

First of all, if I was going out and about in a strange place, where **ya ne rozmovlyav movoyu**[213], I would want to make sure I had the **adresa**[214] of the place I was staying at in the local **alfavitom**[215]. That way people could help me get **dodomu**[216] if I got lost … and I get lost fairly easily! I would also want a way to make contact with my host, if that was **mozhlyvo**[217].

This is our address це наша адреса Tse nasha adresa **"tse nasha adresa"**	Just ask someone просто запитай когось Prosto zapytay kohos' **"prosto zapytay kohos"**
If you get lost якщо ти заблукаєш Yakshcho ty zablukayesh **"yakshcho ty zablukayesh"**	Send me a message надішліть мені повідомлення nadishlit meni povidomlennya **"nadishlit menyi poviye- domlenya"**

---

[213] Where I didn't speak the language
[214] address
[215] alphabet
[216] home
[217] Possible. This reminds me of the words for can.

Second of all, there might be help available for a refugee where you are. If there is a local refugee centre, they will be able to advise about what is available and how to access it. **V Interneti**[218] I can see that there **mozhut' buty**[219] transport passes, access to welfare and services.

If you want to tell a Ukrainian about **vidstan'**[220], their unit of measurement is **kilometr**[221]. Or you can use our old **druha**[222] **chas**[223], to say **skil'ky chasu**[224] it takes to walk somewhere.

This is the supermarket це супермаркет Tse supermarket **"tse supermarket"**	This is the refugee centre це центр для біженців Tse tsentr dlya bizhentsiv **"tse tsentr dle b-ye-zhent-siv"**
Five minutes on foot п'ять хвилин пішки p'yat khvylyn pishky **"p'yet hoolin peeyeshki"**	It is four kilometres це чотири кілометри Tse chotyry kilometry **"tse chotiri kilometry"**

---

[218] On the internet
[219] May be
[220] distance
[221] kilometre
[222] friend
[223] time
[224] How much time

Thirdly, **bez**[225] my car I would want to know where I could get to **i yak**[226]. Are there trains? Are there **avtobusy**? How frequent are they? What is there within walking distance, or do I need to use public **transpotom**[227]? I like being independent. It makes me feel free, and I avoid feeling like a burden.

Buy a return ticket	Buy a day ticket
Придбати зворотний квиток	Купіть денний квиток
Prydbaty zvorotnyy kvytok	Kupit' denny kvytok
"pribati zvorotni kwitok"	**"kupit deni kwitok"**

It is expensive	I am going by car
це дорого	Я їду на машині
Tse doroho	YA yidu na mashyni
"tse doroho"	**"ya yidu na mashini"**

How do you get about?

Walk	пішки	Pishky
Bus	автобус	Avtobus
Train	потяг	Potyah
Bike	велосипед	Velosyped
Car	автомобіль	Avtomobil'

---

[225] without
[226] And how
[227] transport

Guess Test Nine

Look at these words that were embedded in the text in GETTING ABOUT. Try to guess what they mean, and check your answers in the text.

ya ne rozmovlyav movoyu

adresa

alfavitom

dodomu

mozhlyvo

V Interneti

vidstan'

kilometr

druha

skil'ky chasu

bez

avtobusy

transpotom

Record yourself speaking

Record yourself and listen back. Save the file.

This is the supermarket	Tse supermarket
Buy a return ticket	Kupyty zvorotnyy kvytok
If you get lost	Yakshcho ty zablukayesh
Just ask someone	Prosto zapytay kohos'
This is our address	Tse nasha adresa

How do you think these letters sound? Circle the sound for each letter that you think is most likely. Then look back at the alphabet page to check.

		This sound?	Or this sound?
4	Г г	h	ia, ya-
5	Ґ ґ	h	g
11	И и	y	g
14	Й й	y	i, j, y-
16	Л л	l	i, j, y-
21	Р р	r	l
33	Я я	ia, ya-	r

This new alphabet is quite confusing. I am going to have to play with it a lot to get used to it.

Match the threes

Match the words in the Ukrainian alphabet, the transcriptions in our alphabet and the English words. Three per group. A real puzzle!

купити зворотний квиток	p'yat khvylyn pishky
купити денний квиток	kupyty zvorotnyy kvytok
п'ять хвилин пішки	kupyty denny kvytok

Five minutes on foot, Buy a day ticket, Buy a return ticket,

How do dyslexic people copy with the Ukrainian alphabet, I wonder! Copy these letters, and use them in the example words (except the last one, which I am going to ignore for now!)

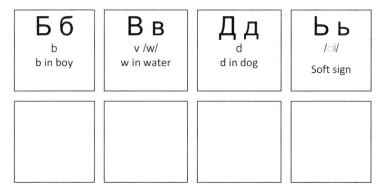

Б б	В в	Д д	Ь ь
b	v /w/	d	/ɔi/
b in boy	w in water	d in dog	Soft sign

End of test.

Network

Tsya informmatsiya[228] is paraphrased from the website refugeecouncil.org.uk.

In the UK the Refugee Council supports Refugee Community Organisations. **Tsymy orhanizatsiyamy**[229] are run for and by **bizhentsi**[230]. They help provide links to refugee communities, so people can connect with others who share culture, **movu**[231] and experience. These networks of people, who have direct experience of what life is like for **bizhentsiv**[232], can help to identify and communicate challenges and opportunities.

Friends	Друзі	Druzi "dru-zi"
Ukrainian people	український народ	Ukrayins'kyy narod "ukrayinsky narod"
Refugee	біженець	Bizhenets'
Experts	експертів	Ekpertiv "eksperchiv"
Help and support	допомога та підтримка	Dopomoha ta pidtrymka

---

[228] This information
[229] These organizations
[230] refugees
[231] language
[232] refugees

Na moment[233] of writing (17th March, 2022) over 3 **mil'yony**[234] people have fled Ukraine since **Rosiyi**[235] invasion began in February, according to the UNHCR website. It is **sertse**[236]-breaking. Ukraine's people want to live **v myri**[237] in Ukraine, with **svoyimy druzyamy**[238] and their families.

As **bizhentsyamy**[239], they will need each other for support. They **mozhe**[240] need you to help them to access the local Ukrainian community, they might not. The numbers are huge **ale**[241] each person's **sytuatsiya**[242] will be **unikal'noyu**[243].

---

[233] At the time
[234] million
[235] Russia's
[236] heart
[237] In peace
[238] Their friends
[239] refugees
[240] might
[241] but
[242] situation
[243] unique

Thank you

My aim in writing this **buklet**[244] was to open up **ukrayins'ku movu**[245] to you (and to me). I am still **absolyutnyy novachok**[246] with this language at the end of this book, **ale**[247] I have more confidence to go forward. I have discovered I like the sounds. I have found lots of **sliv**[248] that are fairly easy to recognise, and that helps. I am even beginning to get a little bit of confidence with the **inshym alfavitom**[249]. I hope I have done the same **dlya vas**[250].

Instrumentamy[251] I am going to use to continue with this language are Google Translate and Duolingo. They are both easy to use, and I don't like things to be difficult.

There is one more section in this **buklet**, a section on **shkolu**[252], which I have written to help people who might find themselves working with **ukrayins'kymy dit'my**[253]. You might like to continue and read this section too.

---

[244] booklet
[245] The Ukrainian language
[246] An absolute beginner
[247] but
[248] words
[249] Different alphabet
[250] For you
[251] The tools
[252] school
[253] Ukrainian children

Dyakuyemo[254] for buying this **buklet**. All the proceeds are going to the Disasters Emergency **Komitetu**[255] to support **lyudey**[256] who really need support. **Dyakuyu**[257] for that donation. **Dyakuyu za chas**[258], attention and effort to learn a little of **tsyu movu**[259]. I wish you good **druzhby ta myru**[260].

---

[254] Thank you
[255] comittee
[256] people
[257] Thank you
[258] Thank you for your time
[259] This language
[260] Friendship and peace

Guess Test Ten

Look at these words that were embedded in the text
in the final sections. Try to guess what they mean,
and check your answers in the text. You will find one
final guess test at the very end of the book.

Na moment

Mil'yony

Sytuatsiya

Unikal'noyu

Buklet

Ukrayins'ku movu

Absolyutnyy novachok

Inshym alfavitom

Instrumentamy

Shkolu

Dyakuyu za chas

Dity[261] are in the business of learning **movu**[262]. (I would say that it's our business too). Even if you don't work **z dit'my**[263], lots of the language in this section is direct, **funktsional'nymy ta dobrymy**[264]. You might find it very useful.

A few phrases for school

There is actually quite a lot here, but if you get to know what is where then **vy mozhete**[265] use it without memorising everything, just by keeping your book to hand.

Ya novachok[266]. This is a place to start. It is about having a go, getting used to some of the sounds. This book is about making Ukrainian feel accessible to you. By trying to use some of this **movy**[267] you are being a role model and making Ukrainian people feel **bazhanymy**[268].

---

[261] Children
[262] language
[263] With children
[264] Functional and kind
[265] You can
[266] I am a beginner
[267] language
[268] welcome

Welcome to our class

Ласкаво просимо до нашого класу

"Laskavo prosymo do nashoho klasu"

Exploring another **alfavit**[269]

Laskavo = Kindly. Ласкаво. Л = L c = s в = v

Prosymo = Please. Просимо. П = p p = r c = s и = y

Do = To. До. Д = d

Nashoho = Our. Нашого. Н = n ш = sh г = h

Klasu = Class. Класу. Л = l c = s y = u

---

[269] alphabet

Ukrainian, one day at a time

Coming in

Hello = Pryvit. "Pryveet"

Good morning = Dobroho ranku.

Come in = Uviydit'. "uvi-yit"

Wipe your feet = Vytyrayte nohy

That is how you do it = Tak ty tse robysh

Welcome = Laskavo prosymo

It is lovely to see you = Pryyemno bachyty tebe. "priyemno bachiti tebe

Don't run = Ne bihay. "nay bee-hi"

Put your coat here = Poklady syudy pal'to

Here = Tut

Look = Podyvys'. "podiwis"

This is your name = Tse tvoye im'ya. "tse tvoye iya"

Clothes

Your coat = Tvoye pal'to

Your hat = Tviy kapelyukh. "tvi kapelyu"

Your scarf = Tviy sharf

Your gloves = Tvoyi rukavychky. "tvoyi rukavuchky"

Your glasses = Tvoyi okulyary

Your shoes = Tvoye vzuttya

Your trousers = Tvoyi shtany

Your jumper = Tviy dzhemper

Your dress = Tvoye plattya

Your t shirt = Tvoya futbolka

Your skirt = Tvoya spidnystsya

Your P.E kit = Tviy sportyvnyy komplekt "tvi sportiwny komplet"

Ukrainian, one day at a time

Creating table

You need an apron = Tobi potriben fartukh

You can paint = Mozhna farbuvaty

Red = Chervonyy

Orange = Pomaranchevyy

Yellow = Zhovtyy

Green = Zelenyy

Blue = Syniy

Purple = Fioletovyy

Brown = Korychnevyy

Grey = Siryy

Black = Chornyy

White = Bilyy. "beerly"

Careful = Oberezhno

Paper = Papir

Water = Voda

Paint = Farba

Glue = Kley

Ukrainian, one day at a time

Scissors = Nozhytsi

It is big = Tse velyke

It is small = Vono malen'ke

It is beautiful = Tse krasyvo

It is messy = Tse bezlad

Don't do that = Ne robit' ts'oho

Have you finished? = Chy ty zakinchyv?

You have time = Ty vstyhayesh. "tivs-tihayesh"

Tidy up time = Chas navesty poryadok

Good boy = Khoroshyy khlopets'. "horoshe hlopets"

Good girl = Khorosha divchyna

Snacks and lunch

Are you hungry? = Ty holodnyy?

Are you thirsty? = Ty khochesh pyty? "ti hochesh piti"

Wash your hands = Myyte ruky. "moite ruki"

A little bit = Trokhy

Is it tasty? = Chy smachno?

Eat it = Z'yizhte tse

Drink it = Vypyty tse

I like it = Meni podobayet'sya tse

I don't like it = Meni tse ne podobayet'sya

It is delicious = Tse smachno

Do you want more? = Ty khochesh bil'she. "ti hochesh bilshe"

Some fruit = Deyaki frukty

Some salad = Trokhy salatu

A biscuit = Biskvit. "bisqueet"

A drink of water = Voda

A drink of milk = Moloko

Not in your pocket = Ne v kysheni

Ukrainian, one day at a time

Say please = Skazhy bud'laska

Say thank you = Skazhy spasybi

It's lunch time = Nastav chas obidu

Do you want to try some? = Khochesh sprobuvaty? "Hochesh
sprobuvaty"

Your fork = Tvoya vylka

Your knife = Tviy nizh

This is your spoon = Tse tvoya lozhka

Your lunch = Tviy obid

Your pudding = Tviy pudynh. "tvi puden"

Your drink = Tviy napiy

Careful = Oberezhno

Don't worry = Ne khvuylyuysya. "ne hooie-yooie-sya"

Let's clean that up = Davayte pochystymo tse

Do you want more? = Ty khochesh bil'she? "ti hochesh bilshe"

Do you like it? = Tobi tse podobayet'sya?

Put it here = Pokladi' tse syudy

Ukrainian, one day at a time

Counting

Zero = Nul'

One = Odyn

Two = Dva "de-va"

Three = Try

Four = Chotyry

Five = P'yat. "pyet"

Six = Shis't. "shit"

Seven = Sim

Eight = Visim. "veesyem"

Nine = Dev'yat'. "devyet"

Ten = Desyat'. "deset"

Eleven = Odynadtsyet. "odinasit"

Twelve = Dvanadtsyat. "dvar-nai-set"

More = Bil'she

Fewer = Menshe. "mine-share"

Many = Bahato. "vahato"

How old are you? = Skil'ky tobi rokiw

Making friends

What is your name? = Yak tebe zvaty

You are my friend = Ty miy druh. "tee mee droo"

We are friends = My druzi. "moi drooyi"

I am your friend = Ya tviy druh. "yat vee droo"

He is your friend = Vin tviy druh. "vin tvi droo"

She is your friend = Vona tviy druh. "vona tvi droo"

Me too = Ya takozh

Come with me = Pishly zi mnoyu

Play with me = Pohray zi mnoyu

Play together = Hraty razom

This is David = Tse David

This is Anna = Tse Anna

Hold hands = Trymatysya za ruky. "trimatisya za rukee"

This is your partner = Tse tviy partner. "tse tvee partnair"

That is kind = Tse mylo. "tse mwi-wo"

Thank you = Dyakuyu. "ja-ku-yu"

Ukrainian, one day at a time

Instructions

Which one do you want? = Yakoho ty khochesh

It's your turn = Tvoya cherha

It's my turn = Moya cherha

Run = Bihty. "bee-hty"

Walk = Khodyty. "hodity"

Jump = Strybaty

Be very quiet = Bud'te duzhe tykhi. "boote duzhe teehee"

Stand up = Vstaty

Sit down = Sidayte. "seeya- datey"

Turn around = Obernys'

Hands up = Ruky vhoru. "rookie voro"

Faster = Shvydshe. "shoo-ed-she"

Slow down = Spovil'nyty

Move forward = Rukhatysya vpered. "roohat-se-su pared"

Stop = Stop

Show me = Pokazhy meni. "pokazhy menye"

Tidy up = Prybyratys'. "pri-bi-ra-tis"

Ukrainian, one day at a time

Write it = Napyshy tse

Copy me = Skopiyuyi meni

Draw it = Namalyuy yoho. "nama-ye-ye yoho"

Look at me = Podyvys' na mene. "pody-voice na me-ne"

Be careful = Bud' oberezhnyy. "bood yo-berezh-nee"

Well done = Molodets'

You won = Ty vyhrav. "te ve-hrav"

Clap your hands = Khlopay v doloni

Hygiene

Do you need the toilet? = Tobi potriben tualet?

Shut the door = Zakryv dveri

Come out of there = Vyydy zvidty. "vweedy zve-yity"

Pull your trousers up. Pidtyahnuty shtany vhoru

Wash your hands. Myyte ruky. "moiti rooki"

Use some soap. Vykorystovuyte trokhy myla. "vekory-stovooty trohe mila"

Turn the tap off = Zakryty kran

Dry your hands = Vysushit' ruky

Put it in the bin = Pokladit' yoho v smitnyk

Show me = Pokazhy meni. "pokazhy menye"

Here's a tissue = Os' servetka

Blow your nose = Vysmorkatysya

Wipe your nose = Vytrit' nis. "voitrit nyis"

Look at me = Podyvys' na mene. "pody-voice na mene"

That's good = Tse dobre

Very good = Duzhe dobre

Feelings

Happy = Shchaslyvyy "shches-livi"

Sad = Sumnyy

Surprised = Zdyvovanyy. "di-vo-va-ni"

Excited = Zbudzhenyy. "zbud-jenny"

Angry = Zlyy. "zwee"

Worried = Sturbovanyy

Brave = Khorobryy. "horobry"

Proud = Hordyy

Tired = Vtomyvsya. "vtom-wisya"

Come here = Khody syudy. "hody sudy"

A quiet space = Tykhyy prostir. "tihi prosteer"

Does it hurt? = Tse bolyache? "tse bo-li-che"

Show me = Pokazhy meni. "pokazhi menyi"

Let's patch you up = Davayte zalatayemo tebe

You are alright = Z toboyu vse dobre

Are you alright now? = Ty zaraz dobre?

Let's call home = Davay podzvonymo dodomu

Ukrainian, one day at a time

Talking and learning

Please = Bud' laska

Thank you = Dyakuyu

I am sorry = Vybachte. "wi-batch-te"

I don't understand = Ya ne rozumiyu

Do you understand? = Ty rozumiyesh?

It doesn't matter = Tse ne maye znachennya

Louder = Holosnishe

Say sorry = Poprosy probachennya

What is it? = Shcho tse?

What is it called? = Yak tse nazyvayet'sya?

(What are you called? = Yak tebe zvaty?)

What do you think? = Yak ty hadayesh?

Wow! = Oho!

Say yes! = Skazhy tak!

Do you remember? = Ty pam'yataesh?

I forgot! = Ya zabuv. "ya zaboo"

What is in the room?

Your pen = Tvoya ruchka

Your pencil = Tviy olivets'. "tvee olivaits"

The books = Knyhy. "k-ni-hi"

Paper = Papir

Carpet = Kylym

Door = Dveri

Window = Vikno

Chair = Stilets'

Table = Stil

Bookshelf = Knyzhkova polytsya

Computer = Komp'yuter

The bin = Smitnyk

The box = Korobka

The toys = Ihrashky

The cars = Avtomobili. "automobili"

The water bottles = Plyashky zvodoyu

Home time

Time to go home = Chas ity dodomu

Take this home = Zabery tse dodomu

Get your coat = Viz'my pal'to

Do you have your things? = U tebe ye rechi?

We had a good day = My dobre provely den'

Come back tomorrow = Prykhod' zavtra. "prihod zavtra"

See you tomorrow = Pobachymos' zavtra

There is your mum = Tam tvoya mama

There is your grown up = Tam tviy doroslyy

He has been very good = Vin buv duzhe khoroshym

Vona bula duzhe harnoyu = She has been very good

Bye bye = Pa pa

Using a little bit of Ukrainian with the people you meet will help them to settle in, feel safe and make friends.

I think it is a real pleasure to try to speak another person's language. I hope you get as much as you give from this experience. I wish you friendship and peace.

Use the video on YouTube to help you with the pronunciation.

Дякую

Dyakuyu

Final Guess Test

How many of these Ukrainian words can you guess at? It is good to focus on the positive. Of the words that you do recognise, how many could you use? The answers are in the final pages of the booklet.

The test is a whopping 107 words and phrases. I would love to know how many of them you recognise! If you would like to get in touch, it's ruth@spanglishfantastico.com. Pa pa.

1	Absolyutno
2	Adaptuvaty
3	Adresa
4	Aktesenty
5	Ale duzhe dobre
6	Alfavitom
7	Anhliys'ka
8	Avtobusy
9	Babusy
10	Movnyy bar'yer
11	Bez sliv
12	Brativ i sester
13	Bud' laska
14	Buklet
15	Chipsy z brokoli
16	Delikatna rozmovathat

17	Demonstratsiya prosta
18	Do chayu chy kawy
19	Dobre
20	Dodomu
21	Druzhby ta solidarnosti
22	Druzyamy
23	Dush
24	Dyakuyu za chas
25	Ekstremal'nyy
26	Emotsiynoyi enerhiyi
27	Fotohrafiy
28	Fruktiv
29	Funktsional'nym
30	Hosti
31	Hrupy
32	Ideal'nym
33	Ideyeyu
34	Inhrediyentamy
35	Inshym alfavitom
36	Instrumentamy
37	Intervalamy
38	Ispans'ku
39	Kilometr
40	Kombinatsiya

41	Kompaniya
42	Konfliktu
43	Kontakt
44	Krayinu
45	Lyudyna vas rozumiye
46	Metodu
47	Mil'yony
48	Miy akt
49	Mody
50	Movy
51	Moya anhliys'ka ideal'na
52	Moya meta
53	Moyimy bratamy
54	Mozhe
55	Mozhlyvo
56	Na moment
57	Na svoyemu telefoni
58	Novachka
59	Paketyk chipsiv
60	Polityka
61	Pol's'ku
62	Populyarnyy dodatok
63	Potreby
64	Praktykuvaty

65	Pravda
66	Roboty
67	Rozumiyesh
68	Salat
69	Sertsi
70	Shkolu
71	Shosta hodyna
72	Sim'ya
73	Skil'ky chasu
74	Sliv yak tak
75	Stolom
76	Stratehiy
77	Stresom i shokom
78	Studentiv
79	Sytuatsiya
80	Transpotom
81	Tse ne ideal'no
82	Tualetnyy papir
83	Typy hramatyky
84	U restoranakh
85	U vashomu domi
86	Ukrayins'ka babusya
87	Ukrayins'ki slova v tekst
88	Ukrayins'ku hramatyku

89	Ukrayins'ku movu
90	Ukrayins'kym hostyam
91	Unikal'noyu
92	V Interneti
93	Vashym aktom druzhby
94	Vehetarians'kyy hamburher
95	Velyki hrupy
96	Vidstan'
97	Voda
98	YA chytav
99	Ya ne perfektsionist
100	Ya ne rozmovlyav movoyu
101	YA ne znayu
102	Ya rekomenduyu
103	Yak hostey
104	Yak turysty
105	Z molokom
106	Z supu
107	Znaydy druha

Answers to final guess test.

1	Absolyutno	An absolute
2	Adaptuvaty	Adapt
3	Adresa	Address
4	Aktesenty	Accent
5	Ale duzhe dobre	But very good
6	Alfavitom	Alphabet
7	Anhliys'ka	English
8	Avtobusy	Bus
9	Babusya	Granny
10	Movnyy bar'yer	Language barrier
11	Bez sliv	Without words
12	Brativ i sester	Brothers and sisters
13	Bud' laska	Please
14	Buklet	Booklet
15	Chipsy z brokoli	Chips and broccoli
16	Delikatna rozmovathat	A delicate conversation
17	Demonstratsiya prosta	Demonstration is easy
18	Do chayu chy kawy	With tea or coffee
19	Dobre	Good
20	Dodomu	Home
21	Druzhby ta solidarnosti	Friendship and solidarity
22	Druzyamy	Friends
23	Dush	Shower

24	Dyakuyu za chas	Thank you for your time
25	Ekstremal'nyy	An extreme
26	Emotsiynoyi enerhiyi	Emotional energy
27	Fotohrafiy	Photographs
28	Fruktiv	Fruit
29	Funktsional'nym	Functional
30	Hosti	Guests
31	Hrupy	Groups
32	Ideal'nym	Perfect
33	Ideyeyu	Idea
34	Inhrediyentamy	Ingredients
35	Inshym alfavitom	A different alphabet
36	Instrumentamy	Tool
37	Intervalamy	Intervals
38	Ispans'ku	Spanish
39	Kilometr	Kilometre
40	Kombinatsiya	Combination
41	Kompaniya	Company
42	Konfliktu	Conflict
43	Kontakt	Contact
44	Krayinu	Country
45	Lyudyna vas rozumiye	People understand you
46	Metodu	Method
47	Mil'yony	Millions

48	Miy akt	My act
49	Mody	Fashion
50	Movy	Language
51	Moya anhliys'ka ideal'na	My English is perfect
52	Moya meta	My goal
53	Moyimy bratamy	My brothers
54	Mozhe	Might
55	Mozhlyvo	Possible
56	Na moment	At the moment
57	Na svoyemu telefoni	On their telephones
58	Novachka	Beginner
59	Paketyk chipsiv	A packet of crisps
60	Polityka	Policy
61	Pol's'ku	Polish
62	Populyarnyy dodatok	A popular app
63	Potreby	Need
64	Praktykuvaty	To practice
65	Pravda	Truth
66	Roboty	Jobs
67	Rozumiyesh	You understand
68	Salat	Salad
69	Sertsi	Heart
70	Shkolu	School
71	Shosta hodyna	Six o clock

72	Sim'ya	Family
73	Skil'ky chasu	How much time
74	Sliv yak tak	Words like yes
75	Stolom	Table
76	Stratehiy	Strategy
77	Stresom i shokom	Stress and shock
78	Studentiv	Students
79	Sytuatsiya	Situation
80	Transpotom	Transport
81	Tse ne ideal'no	It's not perfect
82	Tualetnyy papir	Toilet paper
83	Typy hramatyky	Type of grammar
84	U restoranakh	At restaurants
85	U vashomu domi	In your house
86	Ukrayins'ka babusya	Ukrainian granny
87	Ukrayins'ki slova v tekst	Ukrainian words and text
88	Ukrayins'ku hramatyku	Ukrainian grammar
89	Ukrayins'ku movu	Ukrainian language
90	Ukrayins'kym hostyam	Ukrainian guests
91	Unikal'noyu	Unique
92	V Interneti	On the internet
93	Vashym aktom druzhby	Your act of friendship
94	Vehetarians'kyy hamburher	Vegetarian hamburger

95	Velyki hrupy	Big groups
96	Vidstan'	Distance
97	Voda	Water
98	YA chytav	I read
99	Ya ne perfektsionist	I'm not a perfectionist
100	Ya ne rozmovlyav movoyu	I don't understand the language
101	YA ne znayu	I don't know
102	Ya rekomenduyu	I recommend
103	Yak hostey	As guests
104	Yak turysty	As tourists
105	Z molokom	With milk
106	Z supu	With soup
107	Znaydy druha	Find a friend

Printed in Great Britain
by Amazon

79527359R00068